Novak Djokovic

A Biography of the Serbian Superstar

BENJAMIN SOUTHERLAND

Copyright © 2017 Benjamin Southerland
All rights reserved. Neither this book nor any portion thereof may be reproduced or used in any manner whatsoever without the express written permission. Published in the United States of America.

Cover photo by Christian Mesiano is licensed under CC BY-SA 2.0 / Modified from original.

Visit Benjamin Southerland's website at benjaminsoutherland.com.

ISBN-13: 978-1520928319

Table of Contents

Chapter 1: Novak, Tennis and Serbia 1

Chapter 2: The German Tennis Academy 5

Chapter 3: 2005 Australian Open Qualifier 9

Chapter 4: First ATP Title 15

Chapter 5: Winning the 2008 Australian Open 21

Chapter 6: Chasing Federer 27

Chapter 7: Ranked Number 1 in 2011 32

Chapter 8: Battling Federer, Murray and Nadal 37

Chapter 9: Finally Gets the French Open 43

Chapter 10: Djokovic Versus Sampras, Laver, Federer and Other Greats 47

About the Author 52

Chapter 1: Novak, Tennis and Serbia

Novak Djokovic would survive war; he would be the first person in his family to pick up a tennis racquet; he would dethrone Nadal and Federer—but before that, he was born in Belgrade, Serbia, on May 22, 1987.

Srdjan Djokovic is Novak's father. Sports fans around the world know him as the guy in sunglasses wearing a shirt with Novak's picture on it. Back then, he was a ski instructor and worked in the sports equipment business. Srdjan met Novak's mother Dijana on a ski slope. Novak is the oldest of three brothers in the Djokovic family. Marko Djokovic was born in 1991. Djordje Djokovic was born in 1995. They both followed Novak into tennis.

His family was very athletic and competed in several sports. Skiing and soccer were the sports they preferred, so Novak playing tennis was a surprise. That there were tennis courts built at the Kopaonik ski resort, where the family had a business, was fortuitous. He started playing tennis at four years of age. As they saw his ability, his family encouraged him in every way, including taking out loans for his training, and gave him discipline. Later, when he moved to a tennis academy, his level of discipline and dedication shocked his coaches, as Novak not only took every practice session seriously but also would turn up early to prepare for those practice sessions.

Jelena Gencic had discovered Monica Seles, and at a tennis camp, she noticed that little Novak was a star of the future. She coached him and knew he was not only talented, but even at six or seven years of age, was also prepared for a professional career; and Novak told her what his goal was: "No. 1 player in the world!" Tennis was Novak's future, although he did compete in some skiing when he was young.

Srdjan knew what he was doing as he got behind Novak to make him fulfill his potential in tennis: "Only Novak mattered. All of us, even his own family and his coaches, were unimportant. Everything was done to make Novak achieve what he has achieved today. As soon as I saw a small thing not going as planned, I would go somewhere else, for another coach."

Working for his parents took up a lot of his time, but the location wasn't a bad place to be: a pizza restaurant at a mountain resort. He would serve pizzas and pancakes, and he also got a workout by shoveling snow so customers could come in. In the snow or rain, Djokovic was playing tennis, and he used Pete Sampras as someone to model his game on.

When he was born, the country was Yugoslavia, and wars would result in the country splitting up. More war would arrive to Serbia and Montenegro. Novak would have to be alert for aerial attacks, but he still practiced tennis. One tactic he and his coach had was to play tennis where an attack had occurred, as it didn't make sense for that location to be hit again by bombs.

A large part of his life in Serbia was the Serbian Orthodox Church. He learned not only about his faith but also about helping people, and later he would be involved in many charitable endeavors. In 2011, the church gave their highest honor to Novak, the order of St. Sava of the First Degree. Tennis fans have noticed that he wears a wooden cross. He got that in Hilandar, a monastery on a mountain in Greece. Novak spent time there in 2009: "The only thing we did is pray all day, walk around, do some maintenance, and eat twice a day, at 6 a.m. and 6 p.m. It makes you go back to your roots and back to yourself." Being a member of the Eastern Orthodox religion does have an extra benefit today: when he travels around the world for tennis events, he is cheered on by not only Serbs but also Greeks, Bulgarians and other people who share Novak's Orthodox faith.

Novak was still a child, but he had outgrown tennis in Serbia. He was too good, with too much potential, in a country that didn't have the best facilities or the best coaches to develop his talents. His coach in Serbia said Novak would have to go elsewhere to achieve greatness, and Djokovic set off on his journey to be the best tennis player in the entire world.

Chapter 2: The German Tennis Academy

He was twelve years old when he left Serbia for the Niki Pilic Academy near Munich in 1999. Pilic was very impressed: "I soon realized after a short spell playing against him that he had this incredible will. He was great to coach, particularly because he had what it takes in the places that no coach can reach, into the heart and the head." When first approached by Gencic, Pilic thought that Novak was too young to train, but he soon agreed and Novak and his uncle Goran went to Germany.

Pilic had a successful playing and coaching career in tennis. He had previously taught Goran Ivanisevic and Michael Stich at his academy. Novak would exceed what those two greats did, but at the time, he was a young teenager learning the game. It was tough for his mother, who missed him greatly, especially in his first year away. It was also very costly; the Djokovic family needed to find several thousand dollars a month for Novak's academy stay and his travel to tournaments. In the end, it was definitely worth all the effort his parents put in. On the courts, nobody was putting in more effort than young Novak.

Novak was developing a game style that would eventually have no weakness. It was one where he considered every shot a chance to win the point, and he would become elite among returners in the world; and if he didn't hit the winning shot, his long rallies would result in his opponent hitting an error. His right-handed game produced shots of high velocity, and his two-handed backhand was a weapon few players could match.

Novak took the nickname "Nole." It was just a short version of his name. It had only one letter less but halved the number of syllables. Djokovic was efficient and effective not only on the tennis court but also when picking a nickname. Later, the media and tennis fans would provide him with many more nicknames. He would be The Serbinator, Djoker, Djoko, Nox and The Joker. Years later, if Federer and Nadal were the heroes for the tennis fans, as with Batman and Robin, there was a need for The Djoker to battle against them.

There was success for Novak as he played in tournaments for himself and for Serbia. One win was the 14 & under singles category at the European Junior Championships. Djokovic was wise beyond his years, and as he looked to what he would need in the future, he surprised his coaches by asking them to teach him English. Novak would eventually become fluent in five languages. Pilic may have adjusted Novak's grip on the racquet, but Novak used him and many other coaches to learn even more than just tennis skills. As well as to his family, Novak has given credit to his many coaches, like Gencic and Pilic, and later to Marian Vajda and Boris Becker. His other coaches have also included Dejan Petrovic, Riccardo Piatti, Mark Woodforde and Todd Martin.

Goran Ivanisevic practiced with Novak in 2000. He had been told that Djokovic was a future great, and after playing on the other side of the net with him for a while, Goran started to think that assessment was right. In 2001, Novak was the singles and doubles champion at the European Juniors. Few were working as hard as Novak; he would train six hours a day, dedicating his life to tennis. Djokovic would grow to six foot two in height, and as he grew and his game improved, he started to enter Futures events as a step on the way to the World Tour.

In 2003, Novak met Jelena Ristic. They would begin dating a couple years later. She and their poodle, Pierre, would attend many tennis events over the next decade. Novak and Jelena would marry in 2014.

On the courts, Novak didn't take long to find success in 2003. He also showed rapid improvement. First was a straight-sets loss at the Futures event in Munich. He then lost his next event, which was in Serbia, but took a set from Manuel Jorquera. Novak had the comfort of playing again in Serbia at his next event in June of 2003. He would use that, and his quality tennis game, to win the tournament. Novak had received $118 at the previous two events but got $1,300 for this big win. Djokovic also received a tennis ranking, 768 in the world.

He finished the year with three more events in Serbia on the Futures circuit; one was a loss in the opening round, but he made the semifinals in the other two. Nole started 2004 with a Challenger event in Serbia. He lost in the first round. He competed in more ITF Futures events and kept improving his game and world ranking. Hungary provided some success for Novak; he won the Futures tournament at Szolnok. His first ATP Challenger Tour tournament win came just before his first ever World Tour event. In May 2004, Novak was ranked at 515 in the world and defeated five opponents who were ranked higher to win the event in Budapest, Hungary.

Novak Djokovic was beating older players in the youth tournaments and was also very competitive with quality players in men's matches. It was time for Novak to step up to the highest level of world tennis. He was ranked at 368 in the world.

Chapter 3: 2005 Australian Open Qualifier

The ATP World Tour professional career of Djokovic started in 2004 when he qualified for the Umag event in Croatia. It was a close match in the first set, but eventually, the experience of Italian player Filippo Volandri was too much for young Novak, and he lost 7-6, 6-1. He was outplayed in most areas of the match played on clay but did produce four aces compared to none from his opponent. It wasn't a great start to his career at the top level, but it was the start. It was also the beginning of big money tournaments, and while Djokovic went out in the first round at Umag, he made a bit more money from that than he did for winning the Challenger Tour tournament in Hungary several months earlier.

The next month, in August, he stepped down to the Futures level again, but he also stepped up his game by winning a tournament in Serbia. He cruised through the field in the small event in Belgrade, Serbia. In the final, he defeated Flavio Cipolla 6-4, 6-3. Novak then went to Challenger Tour events in Italy and Germany, collecting two match wins in each event, before once again competing in a bigger and better ATP World Tour event.

His first ever win for an ATP World Tour event match was against Arnaud Clement, at the Romanian Open in Bucharest. It was his serve, particularly his second serve, that propelled Djokovic to victory. He couldn't get past David Ferrer in the next round. The Spaniard was five years older than Djokovic, and ranked more than two hundred spots higher at that time. Things would change over the years. While Ferrer would pick up four more wins over Novak, it would be Djokovic who would dominate him. Starting in 2012, he would have a streak of nine wins over Ferrer.

Next on the list for Djokovic as he learned how to play among the world's best players was to travel. While he had been competing around continental Europe, he had yet to experience touring the world as part of the ATP World Tour. He got his first taste of that in September when he flew to Thailand. Nole went all the way to Bangkok, Thailand, to lose to a player from Holland. Dennis van Scheppingen defeated Djokovic in three sets. It was a temporary setback; Novak returned to Europe, and in November, won the Challenger event in Aachen, Germany.

With a world ranking inside 200 for the first time, Novak finished the year with two more Challenger events. In Slovakia, he ran into hometown hero Dominik Hrbaty in the second round and lost. Hrbaty was ranked 14 at the time. Novak's 2004 season ended in Finland; he lost in the second round to Japan's Takao Suzuki. It had been a successful year, which included winning a Davis Cup match against Latvia, but he had bigger things on his mind, like a Grand Slam appearance.

In early 2005, Novak qualified for a place in the Australian Open, and his reward was to face giant Russian Marat Safin, who was at the top of his game then. Ranked at 4, Safin won easily 6-0, 6-2, 6-1. What Djokovic didn't know then was that he had been beaten by the player who would win the tournament. Novak got experience; he got to see what it was like at the biggest of tennis events at a Grand Slam; and as the total prize money on offer for the event was $6,743,444, it meant he got a useful payday despite losing his match very quickly.

At that time in tennis, the top four players around were Roger Federer, Andy Roddick, Lleyton Hewitt and Safin. Safin beat Hewitt in the Australian Open final in four sets. Andre Agassi was also still a force in tennis; Marcos Baghdatis was a qualifier like Novak but got to the round of 16 before losing to Federer; Nadal was an unseeded player; and Gael Monfils was a wild-card entrant. Novak would return to Melbourne, Australia, many times. It was where he had some of his best wins and also a few tough times.

With a ranking of 177, Djokovic returned to Serbia for a Challenger Tour event in February. He won two matches before losing to Dick Norman. Following two small tournaments, he was back in an ATP World Tour event in Spain but lost in the first round. He then won a Challenger tournament in San Remo, and next was another Grand Slam appearance, at the French Open. Like for many players, clay was not a strength of his game early in his career, but it was on clay that he won his first match in a Grand Slam. Novak demolished Robby Ginepri 6-0, 6-0, 6-3 even though his opponent was ranked much higher in the world at 71, compared to Novak's 153. He lost in the second round to Guillermo Coria after retiring in the third set.

The rest of the year would see Novak competing in many large events, but the biggest were the two remaining Grand Slams. He kept showing his improvement throughout the year: earlier, he qualified for his first Grand Slam; at the French Open, he won his first match in a Grand Slam; and at Wimbledon and the US Open, he won his first two matches at each event. Sebastien Grosjean eliminated him from Wimbledon. At the US Open, Djokovic defeated Gael Monfils and then Mario Ancic before losing to Fernando Verdasco in five sets.

As 2006 began, Novak was ranked inside the top 100, and it was time again to go south for the Australian Open. It was another first round exit, to Paul Goldstein. That slightly dropped him in world rankings but only by five spots. He improved on that at his next event, a World Tour tournament in Zagreb in which he had three wins before losing to highly-ranked Ivan Ljubicic. He then defeated Tim Henman in a match in Rotterdam. After a few more tournaments, he would do something very important, in April at the ATP World Tour Masters in Monte Carlo. It was Novak versus Roger.

Roger Federer was top of the world rankings then; he had turned professional in 1998 and was much more experienced than Djokovic was. The match got under way, and Novak wasn't out of his depth. Federer did win a set to start the match, but Novak got the second, with Federer winning the third. The rivalry of the future started that day. The score was 6-3, 2-6, 6-3. Federer would also defeat Novak later in 2006 at a Davis Cup event.

While continuing to move up the rankings, Djokovic kept showing the tennis world that he was a force, and at the French Open, he made a big statement. He went through four opponents and faced world No. 2 Rafael Nadal in a quarter-final match. Novak lost two sets 6-4, 6-4 and then retired. Wimbledon was a similar story: Novak won his first three matches but then lost to world No. 10 Mario

Ancic. Novak was now in the top 40 of the world rankings, and most thought it would be long before he won a tournament. He won his first ATP World Tour title the next month.

Tennis players have often changed countries during their careers, and during this point of his career, Novak was offered a chance to play for Great Britain. At the time, he said, "It's just rumors. The people were very kind to us after the Davis Cup. We spoke to them. Nothing serious, really. We didn't have any serious conversation about a passport." Tennis in England had much more support than Novak had in Serbia, but Djokovic decided that he was making enough money to continue on his path; and while there were great incentives to move, he was happy remaining as a Serbian player.

Chapter 4: First ATP Title

Not many athletes can say that they not only won a tournament but, later, also bought it; but that is what Djokovic ended up doing. There were several years, and plenty of prize money, in between his first title win and buying the event, but it did happen.

His first ever tournament win as a professional on the ATP World Tour was the Dutch Open at Amersfoort, Netherlands. Novak didn't have a lot of difficulty either; he went through without losing a single set. The July 2006 event saw him defeat Serbian Boris Pashanski, Tomas Zib, Marc Gicquel and Guillermo Coria to reach the final. The first set against Nicolas Massu went to a tie-break. Novak won it and then got the second set 6-4. They were evenly matched at the time: Massu was ranked at 37 and Novak at 36. Combined, they had twenty aces in the match, with Novak hitting nine aces. Novak had his first big event win, and it was done on clay.

Novak joined other famous winners of the event, like Rod Laver, John Newcombe, Guillermo Vilas and Thomas Muster. A couple of years later, Djokovic would buy the event and move it to his home country, renaming it the Serbia Open. The tournament was played on clay in Belgrade. In 2009 and 2011, Novak would win the event.

After his historic first World Tour win, Novak went looking for more trophies. He nearly had one at his next event in Umag, Croatia, but retired during the final against Stan Wawrinka. Novak, later, lost in the third round of the US Open, to Lleyton Hewitt, and after losing to Federer and defeating Stan Wawrinka in the Davis Cup, he saw his second World Tour event win. In October 2006, he won in Metz. The tournament was played indoors. Novak finished the year with three more events. At one event, he lost a match to Wawrinka in Vienna; but then, at another, he defeated Andy Murray in Spain a week after. He then focused on 2007, and he was ready for the new year, as he won the first tournament he played in.

Ranked at 16 in the world, Djokovic played in a warm-up tournament in Australia prior to the Open in Melbourne. He defeated five opponents to claim the title in Adelaide. It was ideal preparation for the Australian Open, and it moved Novak to 15 in the world rankings. Federer and Nadal were seeded at 1 and 2, and Novak was at 14 with

Andy Murray seeded at 15. Marat Safin was the 26th seed.

The 2007 Australian Open started very well for Novak; he had an easy 6-1, 6-1, 6-0 win over Massu. Feliciano Lopez was defeated in the next round in straight sets, and then after Djokovic beat Danai Udomchoke, it was Djokovic versus Federer in the Round of 16. It was a case of the master being too good for the young player: Federer won 6-2, 7-5, 6-3. Federer won 80% of his first-serve points and only allowed Novak a couple of break-point opportunities. At this time, Federer was too good.

Following two ATP events in Europe, Novak headed off to Dubai. He won his first two matches before the Swiss Superman was there again in his way. Novak had improved, and he won two of the five break points he had in the match. He also won a set. It wasn't enough, as Roger won 6-3, 6-7, 6-3. It would be several months before Federer appeared again across the net from Novak, and within those months would be many matches against another nemesis, Nadal.

In March 2007, Novak played two ATP Masters Series events in the USA, and he did really well. In both events, he faced Nadal and Murray, along with David Ferrer and Evgeny Korolev. At the Indian Wells tournament, Novak arrived with a world ranking of 13, and he would move up to 10 by reaching the final. He beat Andy Murray to get to the championship match but lost it to Nadal by a score of 6-2, 7-5. A couple of weeks later, the show moved to Florida, and after Djokovic beat Nadal, by a score of 6-3, 6-4, and then Murray, 6-1, 6-0, it was Novak versus Guillermo Canas. Ranked at 53 in the world, Canas went down to Novak 6-3, 6-2, 6-4, and for the win, Djokovic collected over half a million dollars.

In late April, Novak had another tournament win at the World Tour event in Estoril, Portugal. Djokovic was in good form with the French Open approaching, but in the next two events, Spaniards Nadal and Carlos Moya defeated him in the quarterfinals. At the French Open, Djokovic played very well. Now ranked at 6 in the world, he made it to the last four players in the event. Nikolay Davydenko and Federer were on one side of the draw, with Nole and Nadal on the other. Rafa owned the clay in those days, and he defeated Djokovic in three sets before beating Federer for the title in four sets. Novak hoped that when the tennis moved to grass next, he would have the upper hand.

At Wimbledon in 2007, Djokovic had to fight hard, but he won many close matches to get to the semifinals. The match was tied at one set each, with Nadal leading in the third set, when injury ended the match early for Novak. "I didn't sleep during the night because I had a lot of bleeding and everything, so I was barely walking this morning. I did my best to get on the court, really, because

I was thinking, should I go and play? It was that serious." A blister on his toe added to a sore back forced Novak to retire. The final went to five sets; Federer defeated Nadal.

Umag, Croatia, was a familiar destination for Novak, but the result was not. He was upset by Viktor Troicki in the second round. Viktor was ranked at 176; Novak was the world number 3. It was a shock loss, but the tennis season was about to move to North America, and there were big things ahead for Djokovic.

In August, in Montreal, Novak announced he was elite by defeating all three players ranked ahead of him. Novak had temporarily slipped to No. 4 in the world. At Montreal, he defeated everyone ranked 3 to 1. Novak had advanced through the tournament, and to win the title, he beat Andy Roddick, followed by Nadal and then Federer in the final. He was upset in his next event, in Cincinnati by Moya, but still headed to the US Open with a lot of confidence. He met Moya again there, in the quarterfinals, and defeated him in three sets. Next was another Spaniard, but not Nadal. Novak beat David Ferrer in three sets. Djokovic had made his first Grand Slam final. Federer got him in straight sets, but it was close: two of them went into tiebreaks. Federer won 7-6, 7-6, 6-4.

During this part of Novak's career, fans started to see more of his "Djoker" persona. He became famous for his tennis-player impersonations. He not only studied the game closely to find ways to defeat his opponents, but he also studied many players so closely that he could imitate all aspects of their game. He had their walk, mannerisms and racquet swings down perfectly. But it wasn't just Nadal or Federer; he also imitated Maria Sharapova and many other players, both active and retired ones. He also adjusted his clothing, like pulling up his shorts or sleeves, to look more like the other players, and even used towels to adjust his body shape to imitate Serena Williams.

Novak would finish the year with some big wins, including a tournament win in Vienna and two matches in Davis Cup play. But what many didn't know then was that he and other players had been asked to lose matches on purpose. Years later, Novak would explain what happened: "I was not approached directly; I was approached through people that were with my team. Of course, we threw it away right away. The guy that was trying to talk to me, he didn't even get to me directly. There was nothing out of it." The talk was about getting paid $200,000 to lose a match in Russia, but Novak never played in the event there. He didn't need the money; he made close to $4 million just with prize money that year. Plus, he said that being involved in that was "crime in sport."

Chapter 5: Winning the 2008 Australian Open

As he had already been to a Grand Slam final, there was just one small step for Novak to take, and that was to win a Grand Slam final. It didn't take long for Novak to achieve that; the next Grand Slam after the US Open was the 2008 Australian Open, and Djokovic was in fine form. He went through his opponents in straight sets round after round. Hewitt and Ferrer were some of the players he vanquished. That had Novak in the semifinals, where Roger Federer was his opponent.

It was a different Novak from the one who faced Federer early in his career. He was only broken twice in the match; he won 78% of points on his first serve; and he had more aces than Roger. The first set was won by Novak by a score of 7-5. Novak didn't let up in the second set and won 6-3. It was close in the third set, but Novak won in the tiebreak. This set up a huge Grand Slam chance for Djokovic, as earlier, Nadal had lost his semifinal to unseeded Frenchman Jo-Wilfried Tsonga. For Serbian fans, it was also a big time for another reason; Novak's friend Ana Ivanovic had made the final of the women's event.

Ana explained how long they had known each other: "We met each other when we were four years old. We didn't even play tennis at the time. My father and his uncle knew each other from school days, so we were playing in the sand, and it is just really, really funny to see him do so well now. Then we played some tournaments, some under-10s, under-12s back in Serbia. Then we were travelling together, so it is nice to catch up, and we also have some real memories."

Maria Sharapova won the women's final that year in Melbourne. Ivanovic would win the 2008 French Open. But there was a reason for her to be happy in Melbourne: Djoko won. But it didn't go to plan, as his opponent won the first set. Ranked at 38 in the world, Tsonga surprised everyone by claiming the first set 6-4. Novak won the next two sets, 6-4 and 6-3. The Frenchman was serving big; for the match, he had fifteen aces to Novak's eleven, while Djokovic had the better return game and really dominated when returning his opponent's second serve. The fourth set was very close, but Novak got the 7-6 win and his first Grand Slam trophy. He also received a stuffed-animal toy and a check for $1,370,000.

After the biggest tournament win of his career, Novak had a few letdowns in the matches that followed. He lost a Davis Cup match against Russia when he retired. At an ATP event in Marseille, he lost to Gilles Simon in the second round. Next was Dubai. Somewhere, he struggled because of the heat and the times the matches were played, but he put together three wins before losing to Andy Roddick. Nole won the Indian Wells event, defeating Nadal in the semis and Mardy Fish in the final, but was then upset in Miami as Kevin Anderson beat him 7-6, 3-6, 6-4.

The ATP Masters Series returned to Europe, and it was Novak versus the big two players in tennis over three events. Federer defeated Nole in Monte Carlo when Djokovic retired in the second set. Novak won the Rome tournament but lost to Nadal in Hamburg. Novak didn't have to wait long for another chance at Nadal, but it came on the clay at Roland Garros. Novak had to work hard in the first round. He lost the first set to Denis Gremelmayr before winning in four sets, but then went through all his opponents in straight sets to reach the semifinal. Nadal, the master on the clay, was waiting for him though, and Novak lost 6-4, 6-2, 7-6. It wasn't just clay that Nadal excelled at, however. A few weeks later at Queen's, Nadal again defeated Djokovic in straight sets in the final.

At Wimbledon in 2008, Nole had a shock loss. A few years earlier, Marat Safin was too big and experienced when Novak was starting his career. This time, it was Safin who was ranked at 75 but defeated Djokovic in the second round of the most famous Grand Slam in history. Djokovic then lost in Great Britain, and in his next two Masters Series events, he lost to Britain's Andy Murray. At his next event, Novak would be playing for his country.

In most tennis tournaments, you can't win something after you lose a match. But in August 2008, Novak did just that. It was the Olympic Games in Beijing, China, and while he did lose a match late in the event, that still enabled him to play another match for a medal. Playing for Serbia, he started the event with wins over an American, a German, a Russian and then a Frenchman. If he wanted a chance at the gold medal, he had to get past Spain's best player, Rafael Nadal. This was, in reality, the match for that medal, as the other side of the draw was wide open. Federer was upset by James Blake in the quarters, and then Blake lost to Fernando Gonzalez of Chile. Nadal was too good for Novak that day and won 6-4, 1-6, 6-4. Novak did manage to collect a prize; he went on to defeat Blake for the bronze medal. Nadal won in the final as expected. Federer won the gold medal in the doubles.

The US Open was something that got Novak noticed, and booed. The tournament started well for Novak as he easily beat Arnaud Clement and Robert Kendrick. He was then pushed hard by Marin Cilic and Tommy Robredo. That set up a quarterfinal against Roddick, someone whom the crowd was behind and had mentioned before the match that Djokovic might have feigned injuries at times. Novak won the first two sets, but Roddick got the third. In the fourth set, Roddick was close to sending it to a deciding set but lost momentum with a couple of double faults, and Novak won the match with a tiebreak win in the fourth set. Afterwards, Djokovic celebrated and said some things the crowd didn't agree with. They booed him for this.

Roddick talked about the aftermath of their match: "I was talking trash, and he came out and beat the pants off me [in the match], as he would, but then kind of chirped afterward. So he comes straight [into the locker room]. I went right up to him, had him up against the locker. But then I realized his trainer was a little bit bigger than Donovan and I kind of checked myself." Federer beat Djokovic in the semifinals. Nadal at that time was the new world No. 1, but he lost to Murray in his semi, and then Federer won the final.

To some tennis fans, Novak was a villain. They had a myriad of reasons why they felt this way. Some thought that he called for trainers too often, and that it was a tactic he used to disrupt opponents. It was also said that he lost matches by retiring on too many occasions. Fans were used to the Nadal and Federer show, so some were displeased when Novak came along and defeated one of them, or both, in a tournament. Novak's family were not fans of Federer, and back then, Roger wasn't impressed with Novak and how he would retire from matches: "I think he's a joke, you know, when it comes down to his injuries."

After a few more events, Novak went to China to finish 2008 at the Tennis Masters Cup. He got through the round-robin stage with two wins and a loss to reach the finals. He picked up the winner's check of $1,240,000 after beating Gilles Simon and then Nikolay Davydenko in the final.

Chapter 6: Chasing Federer

2009 was not a great year for Novak; it would have been for most tennis players, but Djokovic didn't achieve what he wanted to. His first match of the year was an unexpected loss to Latvia's Ernests Gulbis in straight sets at Brisbane. Moving south to Sydney, he lost the semifinal to Finland's Jarkko Nieminen. Next was Melbourne, and Novak was in an unusual, at the time, position of being the defending champion of a Grand Slam.

It was not a fun time for Novak at the Australian Open. It was hot and tough, and to get to the quarterfinals, he had to play to 2:26 in the morning to defeat Marcos Baghdatis. Then it was a hot match against someone he didn't really like, Andy Roddick. Roddick won in the fourth set when Novak had to stop playing due to the heat. "I've had some retirements, but I've always retired with a reason and because I felt I could not go on. Today

I really tried my best, but sometimes you can't fight against your own body."

The press had many statistics ready when discussing Novak. He had played in seventeen Grand Slams and had retired four times. At that time, neither Federer, Nadal nor Murray had ever retired when playing a Grand Slam match. It was something Novak would have to address to be the best player in the world, and that would not take long to occur.

The heat wasn't a problem two months later; Novak won the Dubai tournament. He would win plenty of matches but no tournaments for a couple of months. His next title was a special one for him, the 2009 Serbia Open. Novak had moved the Dutch Open to Belgrade, and his uncle, Goran Djokovic, was the tournament director. Novak had a bye in the first round, and in the next two, downed Serbians Janko Tipsarevic and Viktor Troicki. After beating Italian Andreas Seppi, he was in the final. World No. 3 Novak against world No. 179 Lukasz Kubot from Poland. It was the expected result: the home crowd cheered as Novak won the Serbia Open final 6-3, 7-6.

The French Open was a disappointment; he lost in the third round to Philipp Kohlschreiber. Wimbledon wasn't much better, as Novak lost to Tommy Haas in the quarterfinals. Then Federer defeated Djokovic in the US Open semifinals. Five titles and over $5 million wasn't a bad year for Novak, but he wanted a lot more. He wouldn't get it in 2010, either.

It was back to Australia to start 2010, and while he didn't retire, he did not have a good time, and possibly should have retired in a match. In the quarterfinal, he lost against Tsonga 7-6, 6-7, 1-6, 6-3, 6-1 and was very ill. "After two games (of the fourth set) I had to go to the toilet. I couldn't hold on. There was no way. Otherwise I would throw up on the court, just a terrible feeling. When you lose a lot of fluids and your engine stops working, that's how I felt. [I moved] very bad with my legs in the fourth, and especially in the fifth set. I wasn't able to run him down at the baseline, and that was the major problem."

Dr. Igor Cetojevic was one of many Serbs watching Djokovic on television in Europe as he lost the match at the Australian Open. Unlike the rest of the viewing audience, he thought he could help Novak. The doctor thought Novak had something wrong with his digestive system. They would meet in July that year, and Djokovic would radically change his diet. He would eat smaller meals and cut out gluten and dairy from his diet, and while Djokovic would become lighter, he would still be strong and powerful with the racquet.

The doctor would join Novak's Team, the short name Novak had for his entourage of family and staff that helped him, and travel around the world for a year or so.

Since then, the doctor has shared his diagnosis and treatment methods: "I found that he was very sensitive to gluten, a protein present in wheat, one of the most common foods in Novak's diet. He grew up, like so many young people, frequently eating wheat-based foods such as bread, pizza, pasta and pancakes. He was a very good student, following my advice and achieving excellent results."

Excellent results would happen for Novak in 2011, but he still had some success in 2010. While there were no Grand Slam wins, he did get titles in Dubai and Beijing. After getting to the semifinals at Wimbledon, Novak achieved a world ranking of 2. But the biggest success of the year involved no money or anything of the sort; it was about national pride.

Djokovic won the Davis Cup for Serbia. He was joined by Viktor Troicki, Janko Tipsarevic and Nenad Zimonjic, but with Novak winning every singles match he played, he did deserve the credit. The first Davis Cup event was Serbia versus USA, and Novak had two easy wins. In July, right after Wimbledon, Novak won two matches against Croatian players who were both ranked in the top 20. After Djokovic beat Tomas Berdych and the Czech Republic, it was Serbia and France in the final. The location was Belgrade, which was an advantage for Serbia. Djokovic was back to being the 3rd ranked player in the world then, and he first defeated Gilles Simon.

Serbia lost a singles and doubles match, however, and so it was up to Novak to keep them alive. He did that by beating Gael Monfils 6-2, 6-2, 6-4. Viktor Troicki beat Michael Llodra in the last match, and Serbia won the Davis Cup.

Like many tennis players, Novak decided to reside in Monaco. He left Serbia for several reasons, and while usually the big draw is that there is no income tax in Monaco, there were some other points mentioned, and Novak would list some of them: "[Privacy is] one of the reasons I am not spending too much time at home in Serbia because I just don't have my private life. That's what I looked for and I found it in Monaco. I just feel great spending time there." There was still plenty that he missed from his home country, as he stated, "I miss a lot of things [about Serbia]. I miss the food, my family in general and my friends who are back there that I don't get to see that often, but at this moment, I prefer staying somewhere else."

Chapter 7: Ranked Number 1 in 2011

In the Grand Slams since Novak won the 2008 Australian Open, and up to the end of 2010, all but one had been won by Federer or Nadal. Juan Martin del Potro had been the surprise winner of the 2009 US Open. If Djokovic wanted to unseat those two legends, he would have to lift his game to an even higher level than he had been playing at, and that is exactly what he did.

2009 may have been the Year of Federer—he won two Grand Slams and was in the finals of the other two. 2010 could be called the Year of Nadal—he won three Grand Slams. But 2011 was definitely the Year of Djokovic. He started it, as all tennis players do each year, in Australia.

Novak didn't have any trouble advancing through the early rounds of the 2011 Australian Open. In the quarterfinals, he took care of Berdych 6-1, 7-6, 6-1. In the semifinals, he ousted Federer 7-6, 7-5, 6-4. In the final against Andy Murray, it was Djokovic who was the expert, and Murray was just not ready for the big moment. Novak nearly broke his first-service game, and with Murray unable to get a lot of first serves in play, it meant Novak could punish his second serve with great returns. The result was a Novak win, 6-4, 6-2, 6-3.

All the results in events during the first few months of 2011 were Novak wins. After Australia, he won in Dubai over Federer, Indian Wells over Nadal, Miami over Nadal, Belgrade over Feliciano Lopez, and then Madrid and Rome when, both times, Nadal couldn't stop him in the final. There were wins on hardcourt and clay.

The streak would come to an end on French clay. He did win five matches, though, before losing the French Open semifinal against Federer in four sets. Going into Wimbledon, Novak was confident he could get another streak going. He made the final but was made to work for the spot; he had three matches that went four sets, including a tough semifinal against Tsonga. The final was Nole versus Rafa. Up five games to four in the first set, Novak broke Nadal's serve with great forehands and an exciting backhand shot. In the second set, Novak rode a wave of confidence and skill to a 6-1 score. In the third set, it was all Nadal. As the Spaniard won the last game of the set without Novak winning a point, it looked to many that Djokovic might fail. That didn't happen,

Novak won the fourth set 6-3. It was his first Wimbledon title.

Djokovic ate some grass from Centre Court to celebrate. He was very happy with the result: "This is my favorite tournament, the tournament I always dreamed of winning, the first tournament I ever watched in my life. I think I'm still sleeping; I'm still having my dream. When you're playing the best player in the world, Rafael Nadal, who has won two out of the last three Wimbledons and he has always been winning the big matches against me in the Grand Slams, I had to be on the top of my game. I had to play my best."

Next was North America, and he arrived as the world No. 1. He won at Montreal, and lost to Murray in the final of the Cincinnati event. The crowd at Flushing Meadows was his next obstacle. He already had two Grand Slams, and if he wanted a third, he would need to defeat all of their favorite players. It took him five sets, but he beat Federer in the semifinal match. In the final, he faced Nadal. Novak was still at his best and only lost one set, but that was in a tiebreak. The result was Nole winning 6-2, 6-4, 6-7, 6-1.

As Novak's victories kept adding up, the media spotlight intensified on him, and reporters and fans often talked about how he bounced the ball a lot before he served. As many as fifteen or twenty times, the number of times he bounced the ball before serving irritated some players and fans. Mind games are a big part of sports, and if Novak was doing it to get an advantage, it probably worked more than once. People started counting the bounces, and Novak must have as well: "My record was in 2007 during the Davis Cup against Australia. I made the ball bounce thirty-eight or thirty-nine times (before serving)."

It was a great year for Novak. He won $12,595,903. He won 92% of his matches. He added ten more titles to his trophy case. Novak set impressive win streaks, including thirty-one wins in consecutive Masters matches and also a streak of forty-three tennis-match wins. He won a title at three Grand Slams and advanced to the semifinal in the other. He achieved the No. 1 ranking in the world. Novak had it all.

Health was something Novak had on his side. While he did have two retirements during the year, he had seven opponents retire and hand him wins. His new eating system had worked; he had energy that he never had before. Breakfast was about energy: "Your body needs sugar. In particular, it needs fructose, the sugar found in fruits, some vegetables, and especially honey." He would end days with a different requirement: "At night, I don't need energy. So at dinner, I will tell my body, 'I need you to repair this mess I made. Please take this protein and do what needs to be done.'" Novak was ready to try new things to stay in top shape, including the controversial CVAC pod, which looked like a giant egg that he sat inside as it simulated high-altitude conditions and did other things that could build up a body.

Chuck Norris, Jean-Claude Van Damme, Arnold Schwarzenegger, Sylvester Stallone and Novak Djokovic filmed a movie in 2011, and it would be released in August of 2012. Unfortunately for Novak, his scene was left on the cutting-room floor. Unless a new and extended version of *The Expendables 2* is released, fans of Djokovic's work fighting bad guys with his tennis racquet will have to search the Internet for the short clip. Novak went to Bulgaria to shoot the scene, which was part of the big finale to the movie of a large battle in an airport terminal. Having an uncredited part in a Chuck Norris movie could mean Novak has a future on the big screen, as one of Liam Neeson's first appearances in a major film was in an uncredited role in the Chuck Norris movie *The Delta Force*.

Chapter 8: Battling Federer, Murray and Nadal

It was starting to be a trend for Djokovic, starting the season with a big win. He lost less than ten combined games to get through the opening three rounds of the 2012 Australian Open. He then defeated local favorite Hewitt before eliminating Ferrer in straight sets. There were two matches left in the tournament, and that resulted in another ten sets for Novak. The semifinal went for nearly five hours. Novak defeated Murray 6-3, 3-6, 6-7, 6-1, 7-5. That was actually the shorter match; the final lasted for close to six hours. Nadal was after the trophy, and Novak's world No. 1 ranking, but missed out. The result in the epic and record-setting encounter was Djokovic winning 5-7, 6-4, 6-2, 6-7, 7-5. At five hours and fifty-three minutes, it became the longest final match in any Grand Slam. Serbian basketball star Vlade Divac attended the match to cheer on Djokovic.

He would lose semifinals to Murray in Dubai and to John Isner at Indian Wells, but another title was won by Novak as he again dominated the court at Miami. He beat Murray on the hardcourt there before losing once again to Nadal on the clay of Monte Carlo. When the French Open came around, Novak had the chance to become the Grand Slam champion of all four events at the same time, but everyone knew Nadal would be trying to prevent that. For a while, it looked like Novak wouldn't get too far in the 2012 French Open; he was taken to five sets by Seppi and then Tsonga. His semifinal opponent was Federer, but Novak beat him in three sets. Nadal was there, as expected, in the final, and Nadal got the win in four sets.

England had always been the center of the tennis world, and in 2012 its importance was doubled. Not only would England host Wimbledon as always, but the London Olympics would also follow it. Novak was looking to taste success, and grass, again on the biggest tennis stage. Djokovic was ranked as the best in the world, but while Roger Federer was getting older, he could still beat anyone. He got the best of Novak in the Wimbledon semifinal. It was then on to the Summer Olympics. Novak carried the flag for Serbia, and their hopes for a tennis medal. He played against an old foe in the second round, Andy Roddick, and won 6-2, 6-1. In the semifinal, his opponent was Andy Murray, and Murray won 7-5, 7-5. Novak still had a chance at a medal, but he would finish fourth in the event after losing to Juan Martin del Potro in the bronze-medal match. Earlier in the year, however, Novak had received a medal for his efforts, the Karadjordjeva Star Medal, which was presented to him by Serbia for all he had done for his country.

Following Wimbledon and the Olympics, there were still plenty of events for Novak to play in during 2012, and he won four more of them. The US Open was not one of these; Andy Murray got the win in five sets in the final over Novak. Djokovic did win events in Toronto, Beijing and Shanghai as well as the ATP World Tour Finals in London. He finished the year as the world No. 1.

The start of 2013 wasn't a rerun; it was a repeat. He went to Australia and won another Grand Slam. He then won Dubai, once again. He won some Davis Cup matches, as well, and then did something remarkable. Nadal had won eight consecutive Monte Carlo Opens, but he didn't get to nine. Nadal did get to the final, but Djokovic defeated him 6-2, 7-6. That gave Novak the belief that he could win the French, but that didn't happen as Nadal got some revenge and the semifinal win. On one crucial point in that match, Novak ran into the net, and because he touched it, he automatically lost the point. Djokovic didn't agree although it is in the rulebook.

Wimbledon was next, and Novak didn't lose a set on his way to the semifinals. He then lost two sets to del Potro before advancing to the final. The result was historic, but not what Novak wanted: Andy Murray won 6-4, 7-5, 6-4. The US Open was also a similar disappointment for Novak; he got to the final, but Nadal got the better of him and won 6-2, 3-6, 6-4, 6-1.

That final in New York City would be the last loss Djokovic would have in 2013. Novak won the events in Beijing, Shanghai and Paris as well as the ATP World Tour Finals when he defeated world No. 1 Rafa Nadal. Not only was Novak winning tennis matches, but he also got engaged.

There are few tennis players without rituals and set things to do, and for Novak, one big one is drinking water. But even though he plays a summer sport, he doesn't drink what would be expected. "Water is a critical part of the body's repair process. But I avoid ice water. When you drink ice water, the body needs to send additional blood to the digestive system in order to heat the water to 98.6 degrees; it diverts blood away from where I want it, in my muscles." He is also someone who eats a lot of fruit, especially bananas.

Something was different at the start of 2014; not only was there no Australian Open tournament win, but he didn't even make the semifinals. Wawrinka defeated Novak in the quarters, but it did take five sets and the score in the final set was 9-7. After that, Federer beat

Djokovic in Dubai, but Novak got the best of Roger in the final of Indian Wells, and soon after, it was another win at the Miami event but over Nadal in the final. There was minor controversy before that in Miami in a match against Murray. Novak had reached over the net, which was not allowed, to hit the ball and win the point. Murray was not happy. At Monte Carlo, Federer eliminated Novak, but Nole defeated Nadal in the final at Rome.

The next two events were Grand Slams, and Novak would see both Rafa and Roger in the final matches. In France, on clay, Nadal defeated Djokovic 3-6, 7-5, 6-2, 6-4. At Wimbledon, Federer gave it his all, but it was Novak's moment and a changing of the guard of tennis as Djokovic won in five sets with a score of 6-7, 6-4, 7-6, 5-7, 6-4. Novak was also world No. 1 once more.

His wedding in 2014 may have been bigger for Novak than any of his wins on the tennis courts. "Seeing her for the first time in her wedding dress, smiling and walking towards me, she looked like an angel," Novak said of his wife, Jelena Ristic. The wedding at the Sveti Stefan resort in Montenegro was attended by Boris Becker, Janko Tipsarevic, Marian Vajda, Viktor Troicki and other family and friends.

As the tennis season moved to North America, it took a while for Novak to get back into the swing of things. At both Toronto and Cincinnati, he won his first match at the event but was upset in his second. He did better at the US Open. Novak beat Andy Murray in the quarters but was then upset by Japan's Kei Nishikori in the semifinal. Novak finished the year as he often did, with wins and the No. 1 ranking. He won at Beijing, Paris and the World Tour Finals in London. In late 2014, there was another Djokovic: Novak became a father to baby Stefan. Djokovic is a famous tennis name, and so is Stefan.

Chapter 9: Finally Gets the French Open

Doing something that is rarely accomplished certainly makes an athlete stand out from their competition. Novak did that in 2015 and 2016. He won four Grand Slam titles in a row. While not the calendar-year Grand Slam, it was the next best thing.

Novak did get close to a Grand Slam in 2015; he was only one match away. His three successes were the expected ones. He defeated Andy Murray for a fifth Australian Open win, beat Roger Federer for another Wimbledon title and then beat Roger again for the US Open win. It was the clay of the French Open that denied him the Grand Slam. But it wasn't Nadal who stopped him; Novak beat him in the quarterfinals 7-5, 6-3, 6-1. It wasn't Andy Murray; Novak won the semifinal 6-3, 6-3, 5-7, 5-7, 6-1. It was Stan Wawrinka. He won the event over Djoko 4-6, 6-4, 6-3, 6-4.

With eleven titles and more than $20,000,000 of prize money, it was a huge season for him. But it wasn't without controversy. At Wimbledon, there was talk about Becker giving coaching advice to Novak during matches, which is not allowed. That controversy has been going on in tennis for decades.

His other championships in 2015 were Indian Wells, Miami, Monte Carlo, Rome, Beijing, Shanghai, Paris and the ATP World Tour Finals. In the World Tour Finals, he lost to Federer in the round-robin part of the tournament but ended up defeating him in the final.

Nole started 2016 off in style, winning at Doha. The score in the final was Djokovic over Nadal 6-1, 6-2. He then won another Australian Open, which tied the record of six wins that Roy Emerson set in the 1960s. Novak took four sets to defeat Federer in the semifinal and then won over Murray in the final in three sets. There were also event wins in Indian Wells and Miami, and he prepared for the French Open with a quick exit on the clay of Monte Carlo at the hands of Jiri Vesely, winning the Madrid Open over Murray and then losing the final match in Rome to Murray. Novak was the current holder of three Grand Slams, and he was hoping to make it all four.

By saying some things that were statistically correct, Novak got in a little trouble from people who complain about things. He said, "I applaud [the women] for that, I honestly do. They fought for what they deserve and they got it. On the other hand, I think that our men's tennis world, ATP world, should fight for more because the stats are showing that we have much more spectators on the men's tennis matches." The topic was women getting paid as much as men, which is always a controversy, as the money is the same but the men play best-of-five sets in the Slams and the women play best-of-three. Plus, the crowds turn up to see the men play in larger numbers, which is what Novak mentioned.

The 2016 French Open at Roland Garros started with three easy wins for Novak over players who were not in the top 50 of the world rankings. He then took four sets to dispense with Spain's Roberto Bautista Agut but followed that with straight-sets wins over Berdych and Dominic Thiem. Now, only Andy Murray stood between him and four Grand Slams in a row.

After the match, Novak said, "It's a very special moment, the biggest of my career. I felt today something that I never felt before at Roland Garros: I felt the love of the crowd. I drew the heart on the court, like Guga, which he gave me permission to do. My heart will always be with you on this court." Novak won in four sets; the result was 3-6, 6-1, 6-2, 6-4. The last time a player had all four men's Grand Slam titles at the same time was when Rod

Laver accomplished it in the 1960s, although he did it twice.

He did only need two more Grand Slams in 2016 to have the real four-in-one-year honor, but that didn't happen. Novak went to Wimbledon, and after nearly crashing his bike into a vehicle, he was told to stop riding a bike around the grounds when the tournament was on. On the court, he started well with two wins but was then upset by world No. 41 Sam Querrey 7-6, 6-1, 3-6, 7-6. He may not have been able to get all four majors in the one calendar year, but there were plenty of people who thought he was an all-time great of the game.

Chapter 10: Djokovic Versus Sampras, Laver, Federer and Other Greats

If tennis success were measured by prize money alone, Nole would be at the top of the mountain. Matches won, tournaments won, Grand Slams won, match winning percentage, service speed, aces, Davis Cup wins, tennis greatness can be ranked with many numbers. It isn't easy for the experts; they not only have to compare players but also eras and all their differences. If Novak were playing in the 1950s with a wooden racquet, would he still be the top player? Could Novak beat John McEnroe when he was at his best? Would Stefan Edberg, Bjorn Borg or Mats Wilander have played the game with a style that Novak couldn't have defeated?

Career Grand Slams. That is a way to measure how great a tennis player is over all types of surfaces and in all parts of the world. Novak is on that list—few other players have a spot on it—for winning all four Grand Slams in their career. As Djokovic claimed the French Open last to complete the big four wins, he was the same as Don Budge, Fred Perry, Roger Federer and Andre Agassi who also won the clay event last. Roy Emerson completed his four major wins with Wimbledon, while Rod Laver and Rafael Nadal checked off the US Open as the last tournament they needed. That is a short list, and on this, Novak has a claim to be in the top ten of all time, if not a lot higher.

Total Grand Slams. This not only measures ability but also longevity. Having a couple of very good seasons can mean a player gets two or three of the Grand Slams, but to be at the top of the sport for more than a decade is certainly a bigger show of greatness. It is a large sample size; the Australian Open was the fourth Grand Slam to arrive, but that happened way back in 1905. There are very few players above Djokovic on the list of total Grand Slams: the names are only Federer, Nadal and Sampras. With fourteen Grand Slams, Pete Sampras was certainly a very good player for a young Novak to watch and emulate. Novak, currently, has twelve Grand Slams. Active players Nadal, with fourteen, and Federer, the best ever with seventeen Slams, are older than Djokovic, and as they slow down and retire, they could be caught by Nole.

This list puts Novak ahead of so many greats of the sport, and ties him with Emerson who, like Djokovic, won six Australian Opens and twelve majors overall. Laver and Borg ended their careers with eleven. Bill Tilden, with ten, is the only other player to have reached double figures. Agassi won eight, the same amount as Jimmy Connors and Ivan Lendl. How good Novak is can be shown by the players who won only half the amount of Slams: Boris Becker and Stefan Edberg each won six Grand Slams. But that is also indicative of how eras were different, and maybe when Becker played, there were more than the three or four superstars playing, as has happened during Novak's career.

Different eras did have many different numbers of players in the top tier. For Novak, for a lot of his career, it was him, Rafa, Roger and Andy. Sometimes it was only three really great players, as it took a while for Andy Murray to catch up to the other three. Mathematically, Djokovic would have been expected to win one or two majors every year. In 1990, when Edberg won Wimbledon, there may have been more than four contenders in the events. He was up against Lendl, Becker, McEnroe, Jim Courier, a young Pete Sampras, Michael Chang, Petr Korda, Henri Leconte, Yannick Noah, Pat Cash and Goran Ivanisevic. There were at least six huge stars playing then, as well as several others who won Grand Slams. Maybe a reason why Edberg won half the amount of Slams as Novak was because there was more competition, but if Novak were playing at that time, he probably would have been among the top four or so players.

When Sampras was in his prime, around 1997, Boris, Andre, Goran and Korda were still around, and were seeded players. Patrick Rafter, Michael Stich, Carlos Moya, Thomas Muster, Yevgeny Kafelnikov and Richard Krajicek were also top players. Novak would have easily been among the top three or four players then, and probably competing with Sampras for the top spot. Maybe Novak has fewer players at his tier than Sampras did, but maybe Novak has it tougher than Borg did when he dominated tennis around the late 1970s. Bjorn had Connors who was at his level, and young McEnroe was getting there. Other top players then included Vitas Gerulaitis and Roscoe Tanner. Novak could have been getting two Slams a season in that era.

The ATP has a list of all tennis players and ranks them by career index. Novak is on top of that list. He is given the 0.830 result; Bjorn Borg is next at 0.827; and Nadal is third with 0.826. Connors, McEnroe, Federer, Lendl, Laver, Murray and Sampras close out their top ten.

There is a list where Novak is not among the top ten, but with many years and events to come, he should move up from position eleven on the list of all-time ATP matches won. Novak is at 732, 30 wins behind Sampras. Connors is the best, having won 1,256 career ATP matches. Federer is second with 1,080 wins. Another list that Novak tops is that of prize money, with more than $100 million.

Novak is among the greats of his sport. He is also among the biggest names to come from Serbia. Nole is as famous as Nikola Tesla, Karl Malden, Vlade Divac or Peja Stojakovic. Djokovic is a huge success, and after he ends his record-setting tennis career, he will be so popular that he could become the president of Serbia.

About the Author

Benjamin Southerland is a lifelong Chicagoland resident. Southerland developed a strong interest for politics and government during his college years through his study of leaders who have shaped history, such as Winston Churchill, Napoleon, and Thomas Jefferson. Southerland is also interested in individuals who have impacted the world of sports and entertainment. He has studied and written about politicians, world leaders, athletes, and celebrities. He researches these fascinating figures extensively in order to determine what has shaped their worldviews and contributed to their success. He aims for his books to give readers a deep understanding of the achievements, inspirations, and goals of the world's most influential individuals. Follow Benjamin Southerland at his website benjaminsoutherland.com to learn about his latest books.

16771754R00032

Printed in Great Britain
by Amazon